CU00663425

Medicine
Then and Now

Louise & Richard Spilsbury

Contents

OXFORD
UNIVERSITY PRESS

OXFORD
UNIVERSITY PRESS

Great Clarendon Street, Oxford, OX2 6DP, United Kingdom

Oxford University Press is a department of the University of Oxford. It furthers the University's objective of excellence in research, scholarship, and education by publishing worldwide. Oxford is a registered trade mark of Oxford University Press in the UK and in certain other countries

ISBN: 978 0 19 464506 5

An Audio CD Pack containing this book and a CD is also available, ISBN 978 0 19 464546 1

The CD has a choice of American and British English recordings of the complete text.

An accompanying Activity Book is also available, ISBN 978 0 19 464516 4

Printed in China

This book is printed on paper from certified and well-managed sources.

ACKNOWLEDGEMENTS

Illustrations by: Kelly Kennedy pp.9, 14, 22, 26; Ian Moores pp.18, 21, 43; Dusan Pavlic/Beehive Illustration pp.36; Roger at KJA Artists p.4; Alan Rowe pp.36, 48.

The Publishers would also like to thank the following for their kind permission to reproduce photographs and other copyright material: Akg Images pp.7 (De Agostini Pict.Li), 10 (Erich Lessing); Alamy pp.4 (Interfoto/amulet), 8 (Dinidia Photos), 22 (Mary Evans Picture Library), 25 (David Sutherland), 28 (Avico Ltd), 31 (Scott Camazine/pacemaker), 33 (Ulrich Doering); The Art Archive pp.4 (Museo Banco Central de Quito Ecuador/Gianni Dagli Orti/shaman statue), 12 (Hôtel-Dieu Montreuil-sur-Mer/Kharbine-Tapabor/Coll. J. Vigne); The Bridgeman Art Library pp.11 (View of a communal lavatory (colour photo), Roman/Ostia Antica, Rome, Italy/© Gerard Degeorge), 16 (The Heart and the Circulation, facsimile of the Windsor book (pen and ink on paper), Vinci, Leonardo da (1452–1519) (after)/Bibliotheque des Arts Decoratifs, Paris, France/Archives Charmet); Corbis pp.6 (Yang Liu/plants for medicines), 14 (Bettmann); Getty Images pp.6 (Deni Brown/Dorling Kindersley/aloe vera), 13 (De Agostini), 34 (David S. Holloway), 35 (Mitchell Funk/Photographer's Choice); Oxford University Press pp.3, 11 (Roman baths), 21, 32; Pfizer p.23 © Pfizer Inc. All rights reserved. Used with Permission/soldier getting penicillin; Photolibrary pp.20 (Peter Arnold Images), 23 (Anna Schneider/Sodapix AG/antibiotics); Science Photo Library pp.9 (Scientifica/Visuals Unlimited), 15 (Sheila Terry), 19 (G. Tomsich/microscope, Steve Gschmeissner/plaque bacteria), 24 (Arno Massee), 26 (Health Protection Agency), 27 (Chagnon), 29 (Astier-Chru Lille), 30 (Jill Varney); Wellcome Library, London pp.17, 31 (kidney dialysis).

With thanks to Ann Fullick for science checking

Introduction

Today, when we have a headache or a fever, we can take medicine to make us well. When we go to hospital, doctors use medicine to help to make us well. In the past, medicine was different from what it is like today.

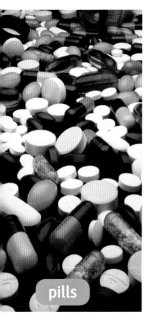

pills

medicine made from plants

cough medicine

Have you ever been ill?

Have you ever been to hospital?

What types of medicine have you used?

Do you know what medicine was like in the past?

Discover!

Now read and discover more about medicine in the past and medicine today!

3

1 Early Medicine

Thousands of years ago, people tried to heal broken bones, but they thought that only magic could cure them when they were ill!

Healthy Nomads

Early people were nomads – they didn't live in one place. They traveled around to look for food. They were healthy people. They lived outdoors most of the time and they walked and ran a lot. They hunted animals and ate the meat when it was still fresh. They usually ate plants on the same day that they picked them.

People used mud to heal broken bones. If they broke an arm or a leg, they put wet mud on it. Then the mud became dry and hard, and it stopped the arm or leg moving so that the bone inside could heal.

People About 10,000 Years Ago

mud

An Amulet From Iran

A Statue of a Shaman From Ecuador

Magic

Early people believed that they got ill because evil spirits were inside them. Many people had amulets – things that people think are lucky. They hoped that their amulets would stop them being ill.

People cared for each other when they were ill. A shaman was a man or woman who sang songs, danced, and did magic spells to make people well. Many people believed that these magic spells worked. In some places today, people visit a shaman for help when they are ill.

Medicines Made From Plants

When early people tasted plants to test which ones were safe to eat, they also discovered plants that cured illness and fever. These plants were the first medicines. One of the oldest books about medicines made from plants was written in China more than 4,000 years ago!

Most early medicines were made from parts of plants, like flowers. People ate the plant parts, or they made them into drinks. Sometimes they made the plant parts into lotions to put on their body. Today, many people use medicines made from plants. For example, people use lotions made from aloe vera plants to make sore skin feel better.

Aloe Vera Plants

6

An Ancient Egyptian Doctor with a Patient

Ancient Egyptian Doctors

We know about medicine in Ancient Egypt because Ancient Egyptians wrote about their world. They cut words into walls and wrote on a type of paper. We know that Ancient Egyptians used magic spells to cure people, but they also had the first doctors. These doctors made medicines from plants, and they were good at putting bandages on wounds. They also used honey to help wounds to heal! This was a good idea. Even today, doctors put honey on wounds because it helps wounds to heal quickly.

→ Go to pages 36–37 for activities.

Doctors and Ideas

When we go to a doctor, we ask, 'What is wrong with me?' Doctors have always had different ideas about how to diagnose and treat people.

Ayurvedic Medicine

Ayurvedic medicine started in India about 3,000 years ago. Ayurvedic doctors ask a patient about their life – how they live, what they eat, and how they feel. To make people well and to prevent illness, Ayurvedic doctors tell people what foods to eat and what exercise to do. They also give people medicines made from plants, and they show them how to do yoga. Today, many people around the world use Ayurvedic medicine.

An Ayurvedic Doctor with Patients

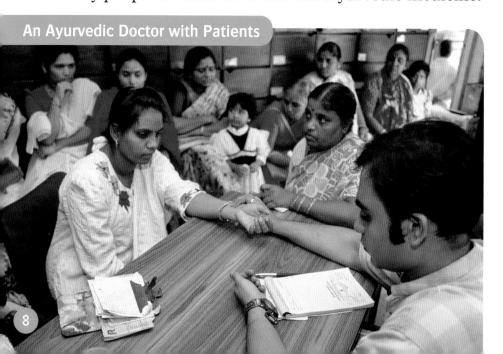

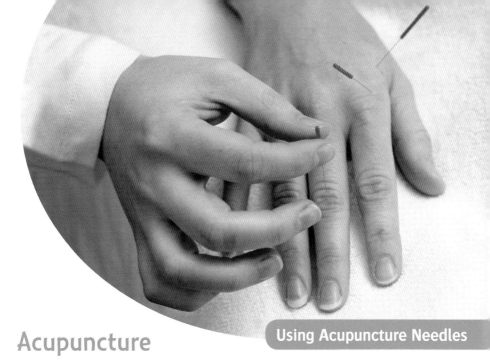

Acupuncture

Acupuncture is a type of medicine that people have used for thousands of years in China, Japan, and Korea. Today, people use acupuncture in many places around the world. Acupuncture doctors put thin needles into a patient's body at special places called acupuncture points. The needles stay in the body for up to 30 minutes, then the doctor takes them out. No one really knows how acupuncture works, but people often use it to treat backache, toothache, and headaches, and to stop people feeling ill.

Discover!

In China, some doctors use acupuncture on their patients during surgery. The patients aren't asleep, but they feel no pain!

Ancient Greeks

About 2,500 years ago in Ancient Greece, many people believed that evil spirits or angry gods made them ill. Hippocrates was a Greek doctor and a teacher. He believed that people became ill because there was something wrong with their body. He told doctors to watch patients and to think about their illnesses. Doctors wrote down what they learned. They made medicines from plants and they wrote about which medicines worked. Soon, doctors started to understand different illnesses. To prevent illness, they told people to eat good food, to rest often, and to do exercise.

Discover!

The Olympic Games began because Greek doctors believed that doing sport helped people to stay healthy!

Ancient Roman Baths

Ancient Roman Toilets

Ancient Romans

Ancient Roman doctors learned that being dirty and drinking dirty water could make people ill. To prevent illness, Ancient Romans built baths and toilets for lots of people to use. At the baths, there were big pools like swimming pools. Every day, Romans went to the baths to wash and to meet friends.

In some places, Romans built giant bridges called aqueducts that brought water to cities from the high hills. This gave people clean water that they could drink and use. Romans also built pipes to take waste away from the cities, to keep the cities clean.

→ Go to pages 38–39 for activities.

Hospitals and Surgery

Today, some people go to hospital to get well when they are ill. In the past, some hospitals were so bad that they made ill people worse!

Hospitals in the Past

From about 1,000 years ago in Europe, monks and nuns cared for patients in hospitals. They weren't doctors or nurses, and they didn't cure the patients. They gave patients food and a bed, and they said prayers with them. The worst disease at this time was the plague. Monks and nuns cared for many patients who had the plague because the patients had to stay in hospital until they died. The plague killed millions of people in Europe and in Asia.

Nuns Caring for a Patient

fountain

An Old Hospital, Syria

From about 1,000 years ago in the Middle East, there were many hospitals. There were lots of doctors and nurses to care for the patients, and they made medicines for the patients, too. Doctors treated everyone who came there, and they taught new doctors and nurses about diseases. These hospitals had different wards for different diseases. There were also pools and fountains, because doctors believed that the sound of moving water helped patients to rest.

Discover! Some hospitals in the Middle East had musicians and singers. They tried to make patients happy!

At a Barber Shop

Early Surgery

Surgery is when doctors called surgeons cut open a person's body to take out, repair, or replace parts. From about 1,000 years ago, barbers started to do surgery. People could go to barber shops where the barbers cut hair. The barbers also pulled out sore teeth, treated wounds from fights, and cut off arms or legs that were badly wounded!

Discover!

In the past, barber shops had a red and white pole outside. The red and white stripes were a symbol for blood and bandages.

Anesthetics

From about 1,000 years ago, doctors in the Middle East started to make anesthetics. Anesthetics are drugs that stop a person feeling pain. Before anesthetics, people felt a lot of pain when they had surgery.

Doctors made early anesthetics from plants. They made some plants into medicines for patients to put into their mouth. This stopped the pain when a barber pulled a tooth out. Later, new anesthetics made patients go to sleep before surgery. When they woke up, the surgery was done!

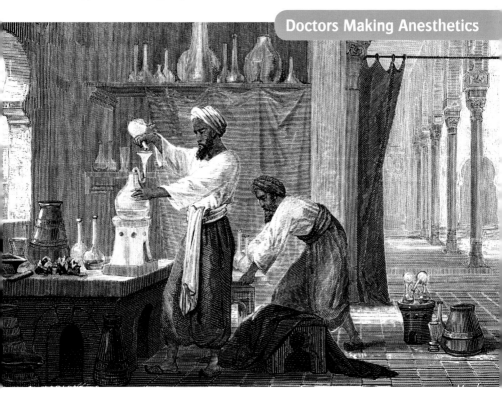

Doctors Making Anesthetics

Go to pages 40–41 for activities.

4 Understanding the Body

Doctors have to understand how the body works so that they can make people well. Understanding the body also helps doctors to cure more diseases.

Looking Inside the Body

Early doctors were not allowed to cut open dead people to look inside their body. An Ancient Roman doctor called Galen learned some things by dissecting animals, but he made mistakes. He thought a person's jaw had two bones, like a dog's jaw. From 1540, scientists started to dissect people's bodies. Leonardo da Vinci was a famous artist who dissected human bodies. He drew very clear pictures of what he saw.

A Picture of Inside the Body by Leonardo da Vinci

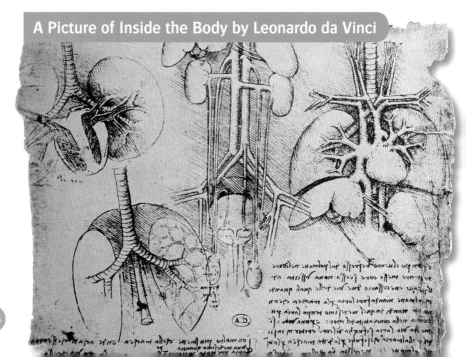

Helping Patients

Ambroise Paré was a surgeon in France about 450 years ago. At this time, many patients died after surgery because they lost a lot of blood. Ambroise Paré learned to tie blood vessels after he cut off a wounded hand, arm, or leg. This stopped patients bleeding too much and it stopped many of them dying.

Ambroise Paré also made the first artificial hands, arms, and legs for patients. He wrote books about his ideas. These books helped other surgeons to become better at their jobs.

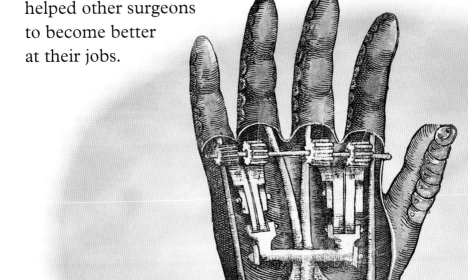

A Picture of an Artificial Hand by Ambroise Paré

How the Heart Works

In Egypt about 760 years ago, a famous doctor called Ibn Al-Nafis studied the heart. He discovered that it moves blood around the body. He also discovered that blood travels from one side of the heart to the other side by moving through the lungs. In the lungs, the blood mixes with air.

Blood leaves the heart through blood vessels called arteries and it travels back to the heart through blood vessels called veins. In 1628, a British scientist called William Harvey wrote a book about this.

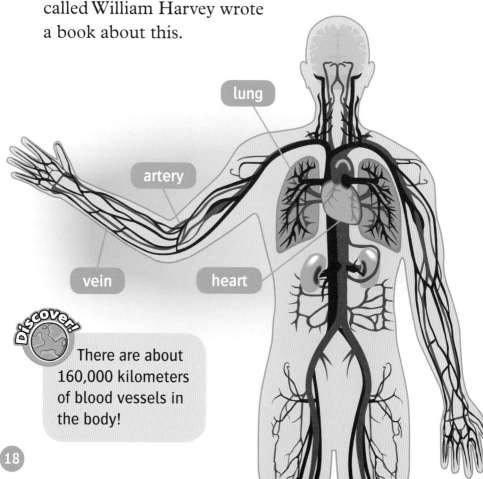

lung

artery

vein

heart

Discover!

There are about 160,000 kilometers of blood vessels in the body!

Microscopes

A microscope is a machine that magnifies very small things – it makes them look bigger, so that people can see them. In about 1640, scientists started to use microscopes to learn about the body. A Dutch scientist called Anton van Leeuwenhoek saw capillaries through a microscope. Capillaries are tiny blood vessels that connect arteries and veins.

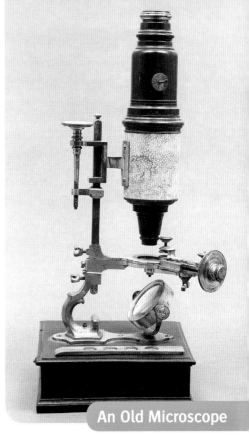

An Old Microscope

Anton van Leeuwenhoek also used his microscope to look at some plaque that he took from between his teeth. He was surprised to see tiny living things in it. These tiny living things were bacteria. Many years later, doctors understood that some bacteria could make people ill.

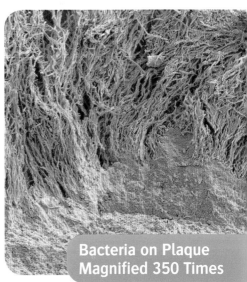

Bacteria on Plaque
Magnified 350 Times

➜ Go to pages 42–43 for activities.

5 Finding Cures

Since 1750, doctors have discovered cures for many diseases. They have also learned how to prevent some viruses and bacteria from making people ill.

Vaccines in the Past

Vaccines are medicines that teach a person's body how to stop a disease in the future. Smallpox is a disease that killed millions of people. In the past, doctors in Asia and Africa put smallpox scabs up a healthy person's nose to give them a weak smallpox disease. This worked as a vaccine on some people, but it killed others!

In 1796, a British doctor called Edward Jenner made smallpox vaccines from cowpox – a disease that cows had. His vaccine stopped thousands of people dying from smallpox.

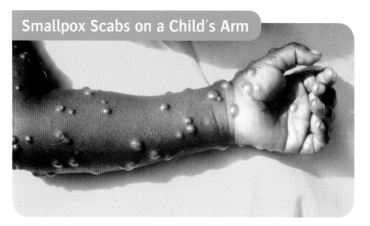

Smallpox Scabs on a Child's Arm

Vaccines Today

Today, doctors and nurses inject vaccines. They use a needle to put the vaccine into a person's arm or another part of their body. The vaccine is a weak type of a virus or bacteria. When a vaccine is inside the body, the body starts to make antibodies to attack the vaccine. Antibodies are substances in the blood that can kill

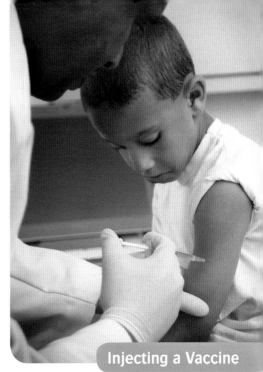

Injecting a Vaccine

viruses and bacteria. When the body has learned how to make the antibodies, it's ready to kill viruses or bacteria when they get inside the body. This prevents the person getting that disease in the future.

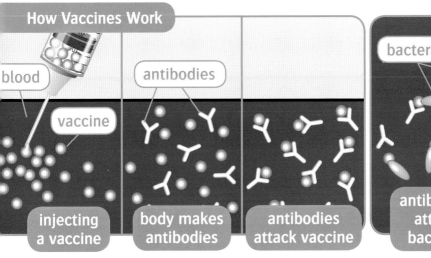

How Vaccines Work

blood

antibodies

vaccine

injecting a vaccine

body makes antibodies

antibodies attack vaccine

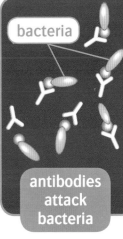

bacteria

antibodies attack bacteria

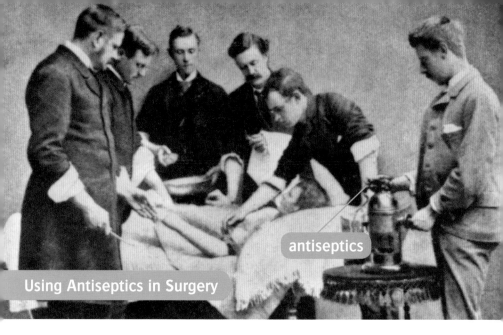

antiseptics

Using Antiseptics in Surgery

Bacteria and Disease

In 1864, a French scientist called Louis Pasteur discovered that bacteria in the air could cause disease. Then he had the idea that you could prevent disease by stopping bacteria getting into the body. A British surgeon called Joseph Lister used Louis Pasteur's ideas to make the first antiseptics. Antiseptics were substances that could kill bacteria on tools used in surgery. They could also kill bacteria that make wounds become infected. This stopped many people dying after they had surgery.

Discover!

When we touch things, we get bacteria on our hands that can make us ill. The best way to prevent infections is to wash our hands often!

Penicillin

Penicillin was the world's first antibiotic. Antibiotics are drugs that can cure illnesses caused by bacteria. Before penicillin, people could die from a small wound in their skin if bacteria made the wound become infected!

Alexander Fleming discovered penicillin in 1928, but two other scientists, Howard Florey and Ernst Chain, tested penicillin to find out if it was safe to use. They also made penicillin that they could inject. Penicillin helped thousands of wounded soldiers during World War II, between 1939 and 1945. Since that time, penicillin has saved the lives of millions of people.

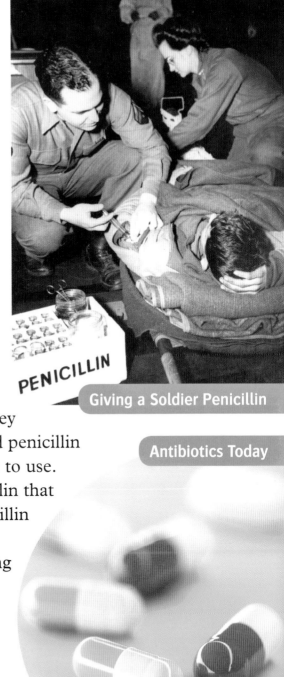

PENICILLIN

Giving a Soldier Penicillin

Antibiotics Today

→ Go to pages 44–45 for activities.

6 Medicine Today

Today, people can use many different types of medicine. These medicines treat or cure many different types of illness and disease.

Many Different Medicines

People buy some medicines from a pharmacy, like pills to cure a headache or a sore throat. Some medicines can only be prescribed, or given to you, by a doctor. Today, there are medicines that cure diseases that spread quickly, and there are medicines that treat diseases that stay with people all their life.

There are also medicines that help surgeons. When surgeons replace a heart or another part of the body, medicines stop the patient's body killing the new part.

Doing Kidney Surgery

A Traditional Medicine Store, Morocco

Traditional Medicines

In many places around the world, people use mostly traditional medicines. Traditional medicines are medicines that people have used for hundreds of years, or longer. Traditional medicines are made from plants and from animals, like insects. For example, most people in Africa use traditional medicines, and a lot of people in Asia do, too. In some places, people use traditional medicines because they don't live near a hospital, or because traditional medicines are cheap. In other places, people use both traditional medicines, and medicines that are made by scientists in laboratories.

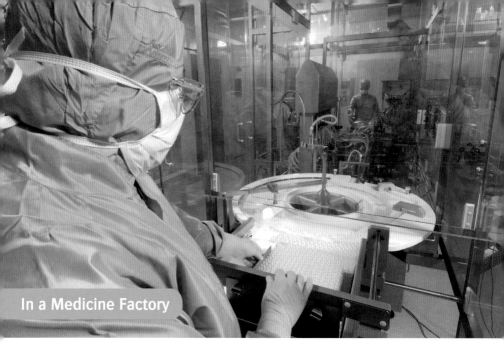

In a Medicine Factory

Making Medicines

The medicines that are made in laboratories and factories are often copies of medicines made from plants. Malaria is a disease that causes fever and can kill people. People can get it when an insect called a mosquito bites them. To cure malaria, people first made a medicine from quinine. Quinine is a substance that comes from a rainforest tree. Then scientists started to make copies of this medicine in a laboratory. Today, quinine drugs are made without plants.

Discover!

Thousands of medicines have been made from rainforest plants. If people cut down rainforests, we will lose plants that could make more medicines.

Testing Medicines

Scientists discover thousands of new drugs every year. They test all new drugs to see if they work and to find out if they are safe for people to use. Scientists also test drugs to find out how much is safe for patients to take. Medicines are tested very carefully in laboratories. Then they are tested on people. Drug companies pay scientists to make new drugs and to test new drugs, and doing these things can take a very long time. That's why some drugs are very expensive.

Testing New Medicines

→ Go to pages 46–47 for activities.

Doctors and nurses give people medicine, and they use many different types of machine to diagnose diseases. They also use machines in surgery, and they use machines to take people to hospital.

An Air Ambulance

Ambulances

An ambulance is a vehicle that takes people to hospital when they are ill or wounded. Many ambulances carry things like bandages and drugs that can be used to treat patients on the way to hospital. Ambulances have flashing lights and they make sounds to tell other drivers to get out of the way, like police cars do. In some places, there are air ambulances, too.

X-Ray Machines and Scanning Machines

In hospitals, doctors use machines to look inside a patient's body. This helps doctors to diagnose what is wrong with a patient so that they know how to treat them. If someone breaks a bone in their body, doctors can take an X-ray picture of it. X-ray machines look inside a person and make pictures of the hard parts of their body, like their bones and teeth.

Scanning machines can take pictures of the soft parts inside a person's body, like their heart and brain. Doctors also use scanning machines to look inside a mother's body to see if her baby is healthy.

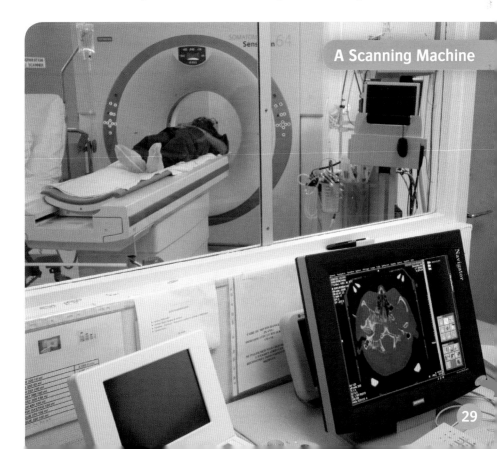

A Scanning Machine

Surgery Today

Today, some surgeons watch television when they do operations! Surgeons do this when they do keyhole surgery. First they cut a small hole in a part of a patient's body. Then they put a tiny camera into the hole. The camera shows on a television screen what is inside the patient's body. Surgeons do the operation using long, thin tools that go into the body through different holes. During the operation, surgeons watch what is happening on the television screen. This type of surgery causes patients less pain and they get well more quickly.

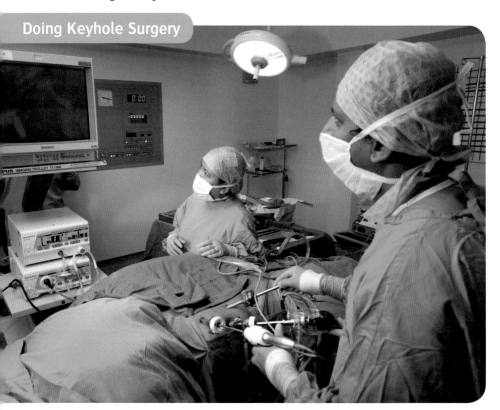

Doing Keyhole Surgery

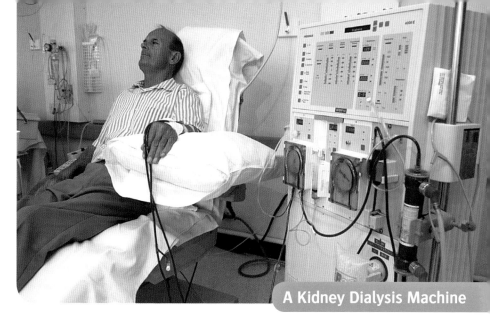

A Kidney Dialysis Machine

Machines That Save Lives

Some machines keep patients alive. Some people use a kidney dialysis machine. Kidneys are parts of the body that keep the blood clean. If someone's kidney doesn't work, they can die. A kidney dialysis machine slowly takes out some blood, cleans it, and then puts it back inside the body again.

Some people have a heart that doesn't work well. A pacemaker is a machine that goes inside a patient's body. It makes their heart work better and keeps them well. Some babies and very young children have pacemakers.

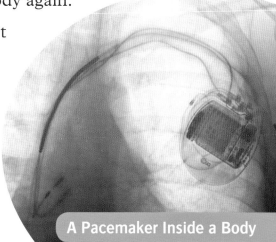

A Pacemaker Inside a Body

→ Go to pages 48–49 for activities.

8 Medicine in the Future

Medicine is very different today from how it was in the past. What will medicine be like in the future?

Living Longer

Medicine has helped people to live longer. In 1900, most people only lived to be about 45 years old. Today, people in many parts of the world live 30 years longer than they did in 1900. Some people say that by 2060, many people will live to be 100 years old!

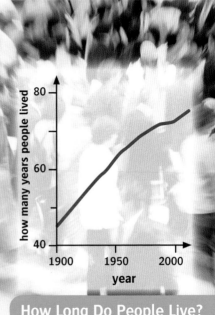

How Long Do People Live?

New Medicines

In the future, scientists will discover new medicines. For example, some drug companies are trying to grow plants with vaccines that people can eat. It's expensive to use vaccines that doctors and nurses have to inject. Vaccines that people can eat will be cheaper and much easier to use. For example, bananas that contain vaccines could prevent many children dying of diseases that can be cured.

Buying Medicines, Uganda

Medicines for Everyone

In some places in the world even today, many people die from diseases that can be cured. This is usually because they don't have enough money to buy the medicines that they need. For example, about one million people die from malaria every year.

In 2009, one of the world's biggest drug companies started to sell cheap medicines to some countries. In the future, hopefully everyone will get the medicines that they need. This could happen if more drug companies sell cheap medicines to poor people.

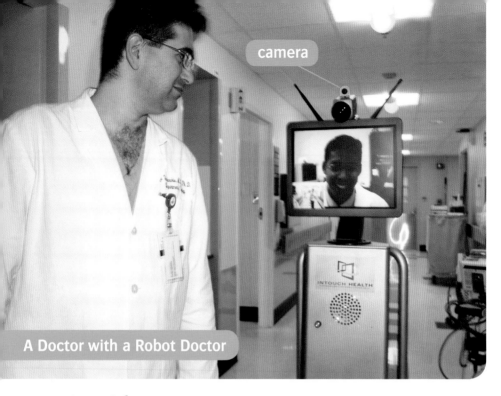

camera

A Doctor with a Robot Doctor

New Ideas

Some hospitals use robot doctors with computer screens and cameras, so that doctors and patients can talk to other doctors at other hospitals. Surgeons also use robots to help them to do operations. In the future, doctors will also use tiny robots called nanobots. Doctors will inject nanobots into a patient's blood, so that the nanobots can move around inside the patient's body and discover what is wrong. In the future, maybe robot surgeons will do operations.

Now, scientists are also developing medicines to help people to grow new fingers and other body parts when they are wounded. There will be more surprises and new discoveries in medicine in the future!

Staying Healthy

The best way to stay well is to stay healthy. Try to have a healthy diet and drink eight glasses of water every day – and more when it's hot. Keep clean – take a shower often, brush your teeth every day, and wash your hands after going to the toilet and before you eat.

Most of us know that exercise helps us to stay healthy, but did you know that people do more exercise if they do a sport that they like or that they can do with friends? What do you do to stay healthy?

Everyone Needs Exercise!

→ Go to pages 50–51 for activities.

1 Early Medicine

← Read pages 4–7.

1 Write the words.

mud   plants   ~~skin~~   bandage
wound   bone   honey   lotion

1 _____skin_____

2 _____

3 _____

4 _____

5 _____

6 _____

7 _____

8 _____

2 Write *true* or *false*.

1 Early people were healthy.   _true_

2 Early people used meat to heal broken bones.   _____

3 Early people thought that only magic could
cure them.   _____

4 Few early people had amulets.   _____

5 Amulets are things that people think are lucky.   _____

6 A shaman does magic spells to make people well.   _____

7 Today, no one visits a shaman when they are ill.

3 **Complete the sentences.**

lotions   plants   medicines   skin   ~~fever~~

1 Some plants cure illness and _____ *fever* _____ .

2 Most early medicines were made from parts of

_____ .

3 People made plant parts into _____ to put on their body.

4 Many people use _____ made from plants today.

5 People use lotions made from aloe vera plants to make

sore _____ feel better.

4 **Answer the questions.**

1 How do people know about medicine in Ancient Egypt?

Ancient Egyptians wrote about their world.

2 What did Ancient Egyptians use to cure people?

_____

3 What did Ancient Egyptian doctors use to make medicine?

_____

4 Why did Ancient Egyptian doctors use honey?

_____

5 What do you use to help wounds to heal?

_____

2 Doctors and Ideas

← Read pages 8–11.

1 Circle the correct words.

1 Ayurvedic medicine started in (India) / **America** about 3,000 years ago.

2 Ayurvedic doctors ask a patient about their **pets** / **life**.

3 Ayurvedic doctors tell people what **exercise** / **job** to do.

4 Ayurvedic doctors show people how to **play football** / **do yoga**.

5 **Many** / **Few** people around the world use Ayurvedic medicine today.

2 Match. Then write the sentences.

Acupuncture is a
People have used acupuncture
Acupuncture doctors put
Acupuncture needles stay in
No one really knows

how acupuncture works.
thin needles into a patient's body.
the body for up to 30 minutes.
for thousands of years.
type of medicine.

1 _Acupuncture is a type of medicine._

2 _____

3 _____

4 _____

5 _____

3 Order the words.

1 many people believed / In Ancient Greece, / made them ill. / that angry gods

   In Ancient Greece, many people believed that angry gods made them ill.

2 a Greek doctor / and a teacher. / Hippocrates was

   _____

3 to watch patients / their illnesses. / Hippocrates / and to think about / told doctors

   _____

4 doing sport / helped people / to stay healthy. / The Olympic Games / began because

   _____

4 Complete the sentences.

aqueducts   baths   toilets   Roman

1 Ancient _____ doctors learned that being dirty could make people ill.

2 Ancient Romans built baths and _____ for lots of people to use.

3 Every day, Ancient Romans went to the _____ to wash and to meet friends.

4 Giant bridges called _____ brought water to the cities.

③ Hospitals and Surgery

← Read pages 12–15.

1 **Complete the puzzle.**

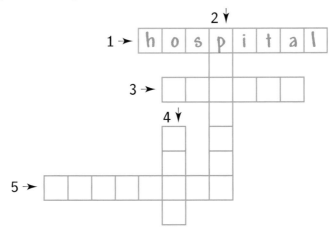

1 People go to ___ to get well when they are ill.

2 In the past, monks and nuns said ___ with patients.

3 About 1,000 years ago, the worst disease was the ___.

4 Monks and ___ cared for many patients who had the plague.

5 Many ___ who had the plague stayed in hospital until they died.

2 **Write** *true* **or** *false.*

1 From about 1,000 years ago in the Middle East, there were no hospitals. _____

2 These hospitals had one ward for different diseases. _____

3 The hospitals also had pools and fountains. _____

4 Some hospitals in the Middle East had musicians and singers. _____

3 **Match. Then write the sentences.**

From about 1,000 years ago	a red and white pole outside.
Barbers treated	were a symbol for blood and bandages.
Barbers cut off arms or legs	barbers started to do surgery.
Barber shops had	that were badly wounded.
The red and white stripes	wounds from fights.

1 _____

2 _____

3 _____

4 _____

5 _____

4 **Answer the questions.**

1 What are anesthetics?

_____

2 Before anesthetics, what did people do when they had surgery?

_____

3 What were early anesthetics made from?

_____

4 What did patients use before a barber pulled a tooth out?

_____

5 When did patients use anesthetics to make them go to sleep?

_____

4 Understanding the Body

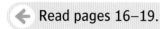 Read pages 16–19.

1 Circle the correct words.

1 Understanding the body helps **artists** / **doctors** to cure more diseases.

2 Early doctors **were** / **were not** allowed to cut open dead people.

3 Galen thought a person's jaw had **two** / **ten** bones.

4 From 1540, **scientists** / **mechanics** started to dissect people's bodies.

5 Leonardo da Vinci dissected **human bodies** / **dogs**.

2 Order the words. Then write *true* or *false*.

1 was an artist / about 450 years ago. / Ambroise Paré

_____   _____

2 after surgery. / At this time, / died / few patients

_____   _____

3 tied blood vessels / Ambroise Paré / part of the body. / after he cut off a

_____   _____

4 This stopped / dying. / many patients

_____   _____

5 made the first / Galen / arms, and legs. / artificial hands,

_____   _____

3 Write the words.

heart   lung   artery   vein

1 _____   3 _____

2 _____   4 _____

4 Complete the sentences.

capillaries   microscope   plaque   veins   bacteria   arteries

1 A _____ is a machine that makes very small things look bigger.

2 Anton van Leeuwenhoek saw _____ through a microscope.

3 Capillaries are tiny blood vessels that connect

_____ and _____ .

4 Anton van Leeuwenhoek used his microscope to look at some _____ from his teeth.

5 He saw tiny living things called _____ living in the plaque.

5 Finding Cures

← Read pages 20–23.

1 Circle the correct words.

1 Vaccines teach a person's body how to **get** / **stop** a disease.

2 Smallpox is a **doctor** / **disease** that killed millions of people.

3 Doctors in Asia and Africa gave people a **weak** / **strong** smallpox disease.

4 This worked as a vaccine on **some** / **all** people.

5 Edward Jenner made vaccines from a disease called **cowpox** / **smallpox**.

2 Correct the sentences.

1 Today, artists and mechanics inject vaccines.

   Today, doctors and nurses inject vaccines.

2 A vaccine is made from a strong type of a virus or bacteria.

   _____

3 When a vaccine is inside the body, the body stops making antibodies.

   _____

4 Antibodies are substances in the hair that can kill viruses and bacteria.

   _____

3 Match. Then write the sentences.

Louis Pasteur discovered	is to wash our hands often!
Joseph Lister made	that make wounds become infected.
Antiseptics can kill	we get bacteria on our hands.
Antiseptics can kill bacteria	bacteria on tools used in surgery.
When we touch things,	that bacteria in the air could cause disease.
The best way to prevent infections	the first antiseptics.

1 _____

2 _____

3 _____

4 _____

5 _____

6 _____

4 Write about penicillin. Answer the questions.

1 What is penicillin?

_____

2 Who discovered it? When?

_____

3 How did penicillin help in World War II?

_____

_____

_____

6 Medicine Today

1 Complete the sentences.

> pills   doctor   surgeons   pharmacy

1 People buy some medicines from a _____ .

2 People buy _____ to cure a headache or a sore throat.

3 Some medicines can only be prescribed by a _____ .

4 There are also medicines that help _____ .

2 Write *true* or *false*.

1 In many places, people use mostly traditional medicines. _____

2 Traditional medicines are made from plants and from animals. _____

3 Few people in Africa use traditional medicines. _____

4 Many people in Asia use traditional medicines. _____

5 Some medicines are made by scientists in laboratories. _____

6 No one uses both traditional medicines and medicines that are made in laboratories. _____

3 **Order the words.**

1 disease / Malaria is a / and can kill people. /
that causes fever

_____

2 called a mosquito / People can get malaria /
when an insect / bites them.

_____

3 people first made / from quinine. / To cure malaria, /
a medicine

_____

4 Today, / without plants. / are made / quinine drugs

_____

5 have been made / Thousands / from rainforest plants. /
of medicines

_____

4 **Answer the questions.**

1 Why do scientists test new drugs?

_____

2 Where do scientists test new drugs?

_____

3 Why are some drugs very expensive?

_____

Medical Machines

← Read pages 28–31.

ambulance   air ambulance   police car
X-ray machine   scanning machine

1 Write the words.

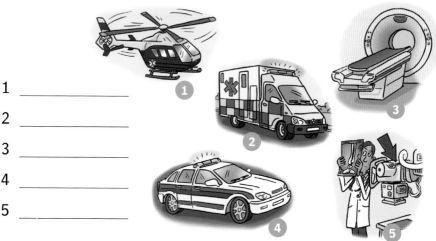

1 _____
2 _____
3 _____
4 _____
5 _____

2 Circle the correct words.

1 In hospitals, doctors use machines to look inside a patient's **bag** / **body**.

2 Doctors use machines to diagnose what is **wrong** / **right** with a patient.

3 X-ray machines make pictures of the **hard** / **soft** parts inside a person's body.

4 If someone breaks a **bone** / **vein** in their body, doctors can take an X-ray of it.

5 Scanning machines take pictures of the **soft** / **hard** parts inside a person's body.

6 Doctors use **scanning** / **X-ray** machines to look at a baby inside a mother's body.

3 Match.

1 A kidney dialysis machine
2 Kidneys are parts of the body
3 If someone's kidney doesn't
4 A kidney dialysis machine cleans blood
5 A pacemaker is a machine
6 Some babies and very young children

have pacemakers.
work, they can die.
and then puts it back inside the body.
that makes a heart work better.
keeps some patients alive.
that keep the blood clean.

4 Correct the sentences.

1 When surgeons do keyhole surgery, they listen to the radio.

_____

2 When surgeons do keyhole surgery, they use a large camera.

_____

3 The camera shows on a television screen what is outside the patient's body.

_____

4 Surgeons do the operation using long, fat tools.

_____

5 Keyhole surgery causes patients more pain and they get well more quickly.

_____

8 Medicine in the Future

← Read pages 32–35.

1 Find and write the words.

m	z	v	x	s	u	r	g	e	o	n	n
e	c	a	g	p	w	t	s	s	n	o	a
d	t	c	h	p	v	d	r	i	d	g	n
i	f	c	i	l	a	i	o	n	e	o	o
c	h	i	k	a	f	s	b	j	r	l	b
i	i	n	l	n	h	e	o	e	y	s	o
n	f	e	j	t	j	a	t	c	t	i	t
e	f	t	m	s	p	s	o	t	n	q	j
z	q	o	p	f	p	e	t	q	p	m	p
d	r	u	g	e	d	n	o	c	u	r	e

1   medicine
2   v
3   d
4   s
5   d
6   c
7   p
8   i
9   r
10 n

2 Write *true* or *false*.

1 Today, no one dies from diseases that can be cured. _____

2 Many people don't have enough money to buy medicines. _____

3 About one million people die from malaria every month. _____

4 A big drug company has started to sell cheap medicines to some countries. _____

3 **Complete the sentences.**

scientists   operations   robots   medicine
nanobots   blood   body

1 Some hospitals use _____ to help them.

2 In the future, doctors will also use tiny robots called

   _____ .

3 Doctors will inject nanobots into a patient's _____ .

4 Nanobots can move around inside a patient's

   _____ and discover what is wrong.

5 In the future, maybe robot surgeons will do _____ .

6 Now, _____ are also developing medicines to help
   people to grow new body parts.

7 There will be new discoveries in _____ in the
   future.

4 **What do you do to stay healthy?**

_____

_____

_____

_____

_____

_____

A Healthy Diary

1 **Keep a food and exercise diary for one week.**

Day	Exercise	Food	Water
Monday	I played football	cereal, sandwich, pizza	4 glasses
Tuesday			
Wednesday			
Thursday			
Friday			
Saturday			
Sunday			

2 **Write about the results. Do you think you should eat more healthy food, drink more water, or do more exercise?**

3 **Display your results.**

A Medicine Quiz

1 Write more *true* or *false* sentences about medicine in the past and medicine today.

Do the Medicine Quiz!

Write *true* or *false*.

1 Ancient Egyptians used honey to help wounds to heal. _____

2 Acupuncture doctors put pills into a patient's body. _____

3 _____ _____

4 _____ _____

5 _____ _____

6 _____ _____

7 _____ _____

8 _____ _____

9 _____ _____

10 _____ _____

2 Give your quiz to friends or to people in your family.

3 Display your quiz and the results.

Glossary

alive living

allow to let someone or something do something

antibiotic a drug that stops bacteria working

antibodies things made in the blood that stop bacteria and other things causing disease

antiseptic something that kills bacteria

artificial something that has been made, for example in a laboratory

attack to fight with someone or something

bacteria very simple living things

bandage something that is tied around a part of the body that has been wounded

become to change into; to start to be

believe to think that something is true

bite to use your teeth to cut through something

blood the red liquid in your body

blood vessel a very small tunnel in your body that blood moves through

bone the hard part of a skeleton

brain the part of a body inside the head; it controls everything that happens in the body

cause to make something happen

cheap not expensive

company a group of people that makes money by producing or selling things

connect to bring two or more things together

contain to have something inside

copy (*plural* **copies**) something that is the same as something else

cure something that makes someone well; to make someone well; to make an illness go away

dead not living any more

develop to think of a new idea or thing

diagnose to say what illness someone has

die to stop living

diet what you usually eat and drink

disease a type of illness

dissect to cut open an animal's or a person's body after it has died

enough how much we want or need

evil spirit a thing that people can't see, but they think that it does bad things

exercise what we do when we move to stay healthy

famous known by many people

flashing when a light is turning on and off quickly

fountain a thing where water goes up into the air

fresh not old (for food)

god some people believe in one or more gods

grow to make or produce

heal to get well; to make well

healthy not ill; good for you

heart the part of the body that moves blood around the body

hole a space in something

ill not well

illness not being well

infected something that is filled with bad bacteria

infection an illness that is caused by bacteria or a virus

inject to put a drug into someone's arm or other part of the body

insect a very small animal with six legs

jaw the hard part of the face around an animal's mouth

kidney a part of the body

kill to make someone or something die

laboratory a room where scientists work

lotion a wet substance that you put on your skin

lung one of two parts of the body that you use for breathing

machine a thing that has moving parts and does work for us

malaria a disease that causes fever and can kill people

medical about medicine

medicine ways of making people well; something that you take when you are not well

monk a man who lives and works for his god

mosquito an insect that can cause disease

move to go from one place to another; to make something go from one place to another

needle a thin, sharp thing

nun a woman who lives and works for her god

operation doctors do this when they cut open part of the body to repair it

pain a bad feeling you get when you are ill or wounded

patient somebody who goes to a doctor for help

pharmacy a store that sells medicines

pill a small, hard piece of medicine

pipe a long, round thing that has a tunnel going through it

plague a disease that kills a lot of people

plaque it gets on your teeth from your food

poor not rich

prayer words that people say to their god or gods

prescribe to tell someone which medicine to use

prevent to stop someone or something doing something

rainforest a hot, rainy place with many trees

repair to put something that is broken back together again

replace to put a new thing back in the place of an old one

rest to do little or nothing when ill

safe will not make you ill

scab the hard, dry cover on a wound

screen the front of a computer or television

shower a place where people stand up to wash themselves

skin the part of an animal that covers the outside of the body

soldier someone who fights for their country

spell words that people say to do magic

spread to go to or to happen to more people

substance a type of material

surgery when doctors cut open a person's body to take out, repair, or replace parts

symbol something that means something else

tiny very, very small

tool something that people use to do work

traditional old; shared by many people

treat to try to make an ill person well

vaccine something that stops people getting a disease

vehicle a thing that you use to take people or things from one place to another

virus a tiny living thing that can make people ill

ward a room for patients in a hospital

waste things that we throw away

without not having something; not doing something

wound a part on your body that is cut or broken

wounded cut or broken

X-ray a picture of the hard parts inside a person's body

yoga a type of exercise

Oxford Read and Discover

Series Editor: Hazel Geatches • CLIL Adviser: John Clegg

Oxford Read and Discover graded readers are at four levels, from 3 to 6, suitable for students from age 8 and older. They cover many topics within three subject areas, and can support English across the curriculum, or Content and Language Integrated Learning (CLIL).

Available for each reader:
- Audio CD Pack (book & audio CD)
- Activity Book

For Teacher's Notes & CLIL Guidance go to
www.oup.com/elt/teacher/readanddiscover

Subject Area / Level	The World of Science & Technology	The Natural World	The World of Arts & Social Studies
3 600 headwords	• How We Make Products • Sound and Music • Super Structures • Your Five Senses	• Amazing Minibeasts • Animals in the Air • Life in Rainforests • Wonderful Water	• Festivals Around the World • Free Time Around the World
4 750 headwords	• All About Plants • How to Stay Healthy • Machines Then and Now • Why We Recycle	• All About Desert Life • All About Ocean Life • Animals at Night • Incredible Earth	• Animals in Art • Wonders of the Past
5 900 headwords	• Materials to Products • Medicine Then and Now • Transportation Then and Now • Wild Weather	• All About Islands • Animal Life Cycles • Exploring Our World • Great Migrations	• Homes Around the World • Our World in Art
6 1,050 headwords	• Cells and Microbes • Clothes Then and Now • Incredible Energy • Your Amazing Body	• All About Space • Caring for Our Planet • Earth Then and Now • Wonderful Ecosystems	• Helping Around the World • Food Around the World

For younger students, **Dolphin Readers** Levels Starter, 1, and 2 are available.